INVITING INTERIORS

INVITING INTERIORS

A FRESH TAKE ON BEAUTIFUL ROOMS

MELANIE TURNER

RIZZOLI
NEW YORK

New York Paris London Milan

For Stanislaw

TABLE OF CONTENTS

INTRODUCTION

My energy and optimism for great style stem from long-held beliefs that we should not only surround ourselves with beauty but also live beautifully. My dad was an intellectual banker by day, and he managed rock bands at night. My mom was the ultimate fashionista. I grew up surrounded by their creativity and passion for poetry, music, and reading, as well as antiquing and spending long days at the beach near our house in Florida. But as much as my parents were free spirits, they were also very grounded. My family immigrated to the United States from Wales in search of new opportunities when I was a child. As a result, my parents gave me permission—and freedom—to dream, imagine, and create. Early on, they instilled a confidence in me to do what I wanted in my own room. Even then I knew that style had to be accompanied by substance— you cannot sacrifice function for form. As a result, my own aesthetic sensibilities are reflective of that dichotomy and appear in the homes I design today. At once, they can be both casual and fancy, simple yet layered, and complex yet serene.

Regardless of style, I approach every new project with zeal—always curious, always seeking out what's new, what's next, what surprising delight waits around the corner. I love embarking on these journeys in decorating with my clients. Over the years, I've discovered that I always

OPPOSITE: A hand-painted wallcovering of statuesque cranes wraps around an oval foyer and brings a touch of the natural world inside. I love the large scale of the birds, especially when juxtaposed with the tall flower-like sconces, which are equally as exaggerated. I'm joined by my two Maltipoo dogs, Scooter and Daisy. **FOLLOWING PAGES**: A striking glass sitting room, part of a new addition, blurs the lines between indoors and out. I designed the low and sumptuous upholstery to keep the view focused on the landscape beyond, while the muted palette takes its cues from the home's understated Mediterranean architecture.

learn the most fascinating (and useful) things from them when we're not discussing their homes. Perhaps it sounds counterintuitive, but the knowledge gleaned from all of our casual conversations—about their families, their travels, even the books they've read—have served as my guiding light. That's not to say that we don't arrive at design meetings with wish lists, inspiration boards, agendas, and a million decisions that have to be made. However, all of those personal and practical details coalesce into a singular vision that allows me to create homes that truly exceed their wildest dreams.

The insights I gather from their everyday routines and rituals also help me create more layered and dynamic interiors. I'm here to hold my clients' hands throughout the process. I urge them to take a deep breath and for us to take a virtual jump into the deep end together. With my guidance, I find my clients to be more fearless and bold in their selections. I'm humbled any time I can remove the fear factor. After all, decorating should be fun!

On the most basic level, this book is about my love for creating beauty. Whether my clients' desire is for a home that is cool and calm or eclectic and colorful, one thing never wavers: everybody wants a place that best reflects his or her self. Today's modern lifestyles demand so much of our energy and creativity, and homes have to go above and beyond simple function to truly nurture us. I believe in the promise of beauty to greet us, comfort us, and envelop us at the end of a long day.

The homes featured in this book are testaments to my clients having big dreams, believing in them, and making them happen. Fulfilling their wishes has allowed me opportunities to explore new cultures and discover inspiring artisans and craftsmanship from around the world. On the following pages, I share the stories of our adventures in decorating, and I hope you'll join me on a design journey of your own!

OPPOSITE: Crystal, gold, and amethyst accents add glamorous notes to a young family's dining room. The fresh color palette keeps traditional pieces, such as the sinuous draperies and ornate carved gilt mirror, from feeling fussy or too formal.

CLARITY

There's something about the juxtapositions of light and dark, masculine and feminine, rustic and ornate, and polished and patina that inspire me. Those contrasts give a lot of energy to a room and often a clearer sense of purpose. Have you ever walked into a space and not known what you're supposed to do in it? I've always been one to embrace the faults of a house. But while I try not to make a home into something it isn't, I do want to make sense of it. Rooms with clarity create a unique sense of way-finding—the connections from room to room are cohesive, clear, and well defined. At the very least, those opposites-attract attributes are harbingers for stylish spaces that need little adornment. I love these types of spaces because what's often left out of a room is as important as the objects I've incorporated. The negative space plays as much of a role in telling the story as the positive (another juxtaposition!), and that dynamic creates a harmonious whole. There's a lot of emotion and, sometimes, sex appeal in rooms with clarity. For cozy, small spaces, or what I refer to as evening rooms—no need to banish the TV—dark hues are the perfect foil to a home's public, light-filled spaces. Richly saturated colors can give profound definition to important architectural elements, as well as elevate their prominence when they're not so special. I often think of simple country rooms where the window frames are painted black. It's the simplest execution, and even without window treatments, the mullions are given a sense of gravitas in the purest form. Since I work on designing city homes, mountain retreats, and beach escapes, I have the opportunity to explore the contrasts of black and white in myriad ways, from wallpaper and floor tiles to art and lighting. There's an element of edginess with a strong sense of verve and a bit of wild amid the soft sophistication. What's still refreshing to me is that such a limited palette seems to reveal countless forms of expression.

REFINED SIMPLICITY

It's important to me to design houses where people use every room on a regular basis. Even in modest homes, people have spaces they never set foot in, which is a shame. This house was designed with a unique trait: there are no hallways. Rooms simply flow from one into the next in what I refer to as a seamless serenity. I embraced the idea, and the design execution allowed me to rethink traditional ways of arranging furniture. The home's most remarkable assets were also the most challenging to work with: the living room, at thirty-two feet long, features a floor-to-ceiling wall of windows. The light coming through the windows gives the feeling of being outside all the time, and hearkens back to the spirit of California living that I wanted to incorporate indoors. Very limited wall space led me to float sofas and chairs in two distinct conversation areas to keep the perimeters clear and allow for passage from one end of the room to the other. By not creating symmetrical groupings, I was able to break up the room in a way that kept it from feeling like a narrow bowling alley.

Since there are no hallways going from space to space, sticking with one high-contrast palette throughout ensures smooth transitions without any jarring changes in mood. That cohesiveness also focuses your attention on the extra-special architectural details throughout, from the dramatic barrel-vaulted tile ceiling in the kitchen to the glass-walled, Deco-style shower in the master suite to each and every light fixture, all of which were selected or designed to be the jewelry of the home. And while those pieces elegantly hover above, I can rest knowing that no square inch of floor space underfoot—whether bleached oak or hexagon tile—is going unused.

OPPOSITE: A striking painting by Todd Murphy is one of a pair by the artist that flanks the fireplace. The dramatic, graphic quality of both pieces helps animate the room, adding a feeling of movement. **FOLLOWING PAGES**: Floor-to-ceiling steel windows run the length of one wall, blurring the line between indoors and out. Two distinct seating areas make the vast, loftlike space feel more intimate. **PAGES 20-21**: Brass accents add sparkle to the library's dark, luxurious palette. Inky grass-cloth walls provide a cocooning effect, while the sensuous curves of the upholstery and cocktail table add a layer of softness. The oversize screw heads on the bookcases are evocative of a motif that Cartier uses on its signature gold Love bracelets.

ABOVE: The bar's open shelving features a mirrored backsplash, which reflects light off the sparkling, vintage glassware and throughout the room. OPPOSITE: The dentil molding was dramatically scaled up, putting a contemporary spin on an otherwise traditional detail. The vertical lines of the Warren Platner chairs play off the lines of the fluted table base. FOLLOWING PAGES: With no hard edges or any kind of trim delineating the wall and the ceiling, the lustrous plasterwork creates an enveloping and soothing environment, allowing one's attention to focus on the furnishings, such as the shaggy armchair, which has an artful, sculptural sensibility, and the bold yet ethereal painting, which enhances a sense of calm.

PREVIOUS PAGES: Every surface in the airy kitchen is swathed in just one of three materials—subway tiles, marble, or hardwood—for maximum impact. The tiles' glossy surface adds a luminous quality to the stunning barrel-vaulted ceiling, which is accented with Sputnik-style light fixtures. Two live-edge walnut tables are spaced gently apart, allowing guests to easily access the middle section of the twelve-foot-long banquette. **ABOVE**: A wall of windows in the master bath creates the feeling of showering outdoors. A built-in shade affords privacy when needed. **OPPOSITE**: A deep, mirrored cast-iron soaking tub, flanked by his-and-hers vanities, is an indulgent, sybaritic touch.

MODERN HEIRLOOM

I often work on houses that have multiple personalities. Over the years, various renovations can transform a home into a hodgepodge of styles. It's often my job to dissect the old additions and put the house back together in a way that makes sense. At this home, a residence that had been previously renovated for an owner with modern sensibilities, my goal was to soften the edges and make it more livable for today's families. The architect decided to keep the home's contemporary rear exterior, but transformed the front facade into something more welcoming and gracious. Inside, I melded the best of both worlds, fusing the contemporary with the classic. The breathtaking master bedroom, at twenty-six feet square with twelve-foot ceilings, is encapsulated in glass like a cube and was retained as my inspiration for the rest of the home's renovation and decoration. More walls of iron windows were added for extra light, and hefty materials such as bronze, marble, iron, and brass were incorporated throughout to play up the robust interior architecture. The crisp vertical lines of the entry's plaster walls add texture and make the space feel taller. In the kitchen, everything is neatly tucked away behind bespoke cabinetry. Even the dining room's iconic Saarinen table has architectural pedigree. However, softer touches, like a hint of blue in each room for continuity, a gallery wall of art hung salon-style, dazzling mirrored surfaces, cozy Moroccan rugs, and bouclé fabrics take the edge off. Now there's even wall-to-wall carpeting to ground that soaring bedroom. For a house that could have ended up being a riotous amalgamation of ideas, I'm proud of harnessing the disparate elements into a singular point of view—and one that's crystal clear.

OPPOSITE: An oversize steel-and-glass pivot entry door set into an otherwise traditional facade offers a hint of the contemporary design to be discovered within. Handcrafted plaster walls in a vertical fluted pattern enhance a sense of height, while the soft Moroccan rug underfoot offers the first touch of blue—a unifying color that appears throughout the home. **FOLLOWING PAGES**: The living room was originally sunken, but I had it raised to the same level as the rest of the house, allowing for easier access to the open kitchen and spaces beyond. A mix of burnished finishes and antique mirrored surfaces add notes of glamour. I particularly love how the lines of the leather-strapped chairs and stripes in the rug echo the grid of windows.

The personality of a space is often defined by its quirks. Hanging the art in an eclectic manner brings a touch of informality to the room's linear architecture.

OPPOSITE: Figurative and abstract art arranged in an irregular pattern enhances the living room's casual feeling and also allows new pieces to be added one at a time. Gilt and black frames unify the composition. The seven-armed sconce radiating off the wall is actually a ceiling light that has been repurposed for this arrangement. **FOLLOWING PAGES:** The lighting fixtures in the breakfast area (left) and dining room (right) add architectural interest to their respective spaces. The pair on the left were inspired by a pair of earrings once worn by actress Elizabeth Taylor. To counterbalance the angularity of the home's architecture, almost all of the furnishings have curved or rounded edges for softness. The silhouettes of the snakes depicted in the artworks on the right are echoed on the host's dining chairs; any repetition of form on disparate objects helps to unify a room.

Large commercial-style cooking ranges are so often the focal point of kitchens. Here, I chose to hide most of the appliances behind custom cabinetry stained in a warm pecan finish. A recessed cooking alcove swathed in marble becomes the room's centerpiece; a generous ledge allows for the rotation of oils, spices, utensils—even art! The vent hood is seamlessly integrated into the area above it. Circular counter stools and a striking lighting fixture composed of bubbly orbs counteract the room's strong angularity while playing into an overall geometric composition.

ABOVE: Wall-to-wall wool carpeting and dramatic sheer curtains add plushness to the master bedroom, which is surrounded by large expanses of glass that frame beautiful views. Although this home is in an urban area, it feels a world away with its lush manicured gardens. **OPPOSITE**: I intentionally kept the furnishings low to the ground to accentuate the dramatic ceiling height. Black accents help to ground the space: the dark fireplace surround is created from Venetian plaster, and the bed is upholstered in a zippy flame-stitched pattern. I rarely use printed fabrics, but the lines in this design reflect those found in the home's modern architecture.

NATURAL CONTRAST

This project, a fun weekend retreat near the ocean, was created for a family with four children, keeping in mind that its prime beachfront location would be a popular gathering spot for entertaining and hosting friends and extended family. Knowing the energy that would be pulsating through the spaces, I wanted to do something bold that would echo their vivacious and contagious spirits. A crisp black-and-white palette is balanced with nubby seagrass rugs, rustic reclaimed beams, and an assortment of woven baskets used as both art on the walls and lighting above.

All of the dark hues are tempered by cool, blond finishes on the wood floors, cabinetry, and even the simple matchstick blinds that filter the midday sun. Adjoining kitchens can accommodate two or twenty, and the rear one, which serves as a scullery, keeps dirty dishes out of sight until cleanup time. In the private spaces, bedside hanging pendants recall jellyfish or sea urchins, and an artist's mural printed on wallpaper echoes the waves of the sea just beyond. The idea was to create an escapist design that was not cloying in its scheme; rather, it would bring home all of the dreamy thoughts of wanderlust under one roof and make them meaningful for both old and young alike—no passport required.

Richly sculpted ceramics, a humble tree branch, and African textiles on the ottomans imbue the entry with an earthy, organic sensibility. Although it is vintage, the black-and-white photograph has a contemporary feel and offers a nod to the home's beachside location. The amusing subject adds a bit of whimsy, which seems most welcome and appropriate at a relaxed vacation-home getaway.

Reducing visual clutter brings clarity to a space. By choosing a banquette to anchor the dining area, fewer chairs were required.

I love mixing various geometric shapes and experimenting with scale. In the dining area, the circular motif on the rattan chairs and pendant fixture is a playful counterpoint to the framed geometric prints on the wall. The banquette is upholstered in vinyl to stand up to the rigors of beachside living, which include wet bathing suits and sand.

An open-concept floor plan is conducive to a weekend house, where everyone can gather together. A scullery, located behind the industrial-style iron windows, offers space for meal preparation out of sight, as well as additional storage. To keep the white walls and upholstery from feeling too cold, I incorporated natural and blond finishes whenever possible, which gives the room a feeling of earthiness. The raw, exposed beams add warmth, patina, and a sense of history.

Each of the concrete tiles in the scullery was placed individually. I chose to run the pattern from the counter all the way to the ceiling for maximum visual impact. The warm brass accents on the range and faucet are traditional touches that balance out the kitchen's contemporary notes, such as the crisp waterfall edge detailing on the marble countertops.

ABOVE: A rustic driftwood-framed mirror is the perfect foil to the abstract pattern of the powder room's graffiti-style wallpaper. **OPPOSITE**: A floating vanity frees up floor space and makes a room feel larger. The blond finish on the cabinetry complements the pale wood floors. A grouping of African baskets, reflected in one of two oyster shell–framed mirrors, counterbalances the linearity of the cabinetry. **FOLLOWING PAGES**: A graphically strong yet playful black-and-white wallpaper we designed is a wink to the dunes and waves of the nearby ocean, while the bedside pendant fixtures summon associations with aquatic life forms such as jellyfish or sea urchins.

COLORFUL

Rules are meant to be broken, especially when it comes to decorating with color. But before I start designing a home's color scheme, I take a lot of time to discover how my client responds to it. Color is a very personal preference, and I'm never one to push palettes that don't resonate.

Often clients immediately shy away from color in their homes, but once I dig deeper and review their wardrobes and artwork, I find ways to link together seemingly disparate threads in a way that ensures they feel totally comfortable with my suggestions. It might seem odd to comb through someone's closet for inspiration, but it works—the most unexpected touchstones are the common denominators. A recurring hint of red on scarves or handbags, or the repetition of green on a tie or favorite necklace, might not influence an entire room, but a throw pillow or powder room is fair game and allows for subtle gestures if there's real resistance.

After all, color is supposed to evoke joy, complement the home-owners, and add character to a space. If it can't do that, there's no point in exploring the countless options and myriad combinations, as inspiring as they may be.

I don't set out to design rooms around a piece of artwork or a rug, but with some renovations, I have found ways to make great pieces shine in what were otherwise inappropriate or lukewarm surroundings that regaled them to second-tier status. By massing a client's cherished collections together—or helping him or her start one from scratch—I can create a very personal color story, especially when the items had been previously scattered around the house and had no presence whatsoever. En masse, the effect can be dazzling.

But regardless of how I choose to use color, there is always the sense that, even in the most formal or classical spaces, one is meant to actually live there, today, in the moment—whether it's the playfulness that comes from a wild tiger print used judiciously on a sofa (or lightly on a throw pillow) or the relaxed feeling that comes from a flouncy 1940s-inspired settee upholstered in an unexpected and electric chartreuse silk velvet. Sometimes, I just use a boost of color on the ceiling, which I consider a room's sixth plane and, more often than not, one that is greatly underutilized. However I implement it, one thing remains true: live with a color, whether a hint of it or a room full, for at least a day and see how you feel in the morning—and never say never! You might be surprised.

A COLORFUL LIFE

When clients want to live with color in a big way, I jump at the chance to facilitate the transition from dream to reality. A palette of sage greens, rosy apricots, and peachy salmon hues were the perfect fit for this family's historic house, which is blessed with gorgeous natural daylight streaming into the rooms for most of the day. The colors are intense enough to define a space, but they don't overpower; they're suited for the family's modern way of living amid rooms filled with classical moldings and details.

I also wanted the perfect foil to show off the owners' antique family heirlooms in a fresh way. And with school-age children, the house is imbued with a youthful energy. The wide front hall is used for impromptu ballet performances by the couple's daughters, so I refrained from adding a rug and created a stylish backdrop worthy of their pirouettes and pointe shoes with a chinoiserie wallpaper and a scalloped-back green settee (no doubt the best seats in the house).

Even on the gloomiest, grayest days of winter, all of the rooms emit a welcoming glow, and the owners' hand is evident at every turn. In the library, where a unique abstract painting was found for a tight space, their collection of colorful scrapbooks was the perfect solution for filling the surrounding bookcases, so much so that they look like an artist's installation. No doubt they're ready to be filled with new memories from their colorful life in this loving house.

OPPOSITE: In this light-filled foyer, a scenic wallpaper melds iconic chinoiserie motifs with the romance of an English garden. Its soothing aqua background strikes a note of optimism, which carries throughout the house. Here, I eschewed placing a rug in the entry to allow space for impromptu ballet performances, a favorite pastime of the owners' children. **FOLLOWING PAGES, LEFT**: When clients inherit antiques from their parents and grandparents, that doesn't mean they want to live the same lifestyle. In every room, it was important to create a lively backdrop for this family's collection of cherished heirloom pieces. **FOLLOWING PAGES, RIGHT**: Since the settee is the first piece of furniture that greets guests, I chose to cover it in a peppy chartreuse velvet to strike a cheerful note immediately upon arrival.

Color truly affects the soul in a meaningful way, and we're naturally drawn to it. Besides defining a particular space, color can also entice people to move from one room to the next.

OPPOSITE: All of the living room's classical detailing, including the decorative moldings, ornate fireplace mantel, and crystal sconces, feels newly fresh when swaddled in hues of peach and apricot. The painting is by America Martin. **FOLLOWING PAGES**: Since many of the rooms receive an abundance of natural daylight throughout the day, I chose colors that would give the rooms a near-constant rosy disposition. At certain moments, they literally seem to glow, beckoning you into the space. The antique oil paintings of the client's ancestors feel fresher when grouped with contemporary figurative paintings.

In lieu of a piece of artwork, I chose to place a mirrored folding screen behind the sofa to reflect light throughout the room. The two chairs framing the sofa have a midcentury vibe, and I chose contemporary upholstery to complement that quality. I find that mixing furnishings from different eras helps keep a room from becoming dated.

Use color in a home to evoke joy,
complement the inhabitants,
and add character to a room.
In both big and small gestures,
color is a great unifier.

The dining room's colorful abstract painting is certainly an attention grabber, but subtle details, when applied correctly, can have an equally dramatic impact. The contrasting magenta trim that outlines the chairbacks and seat cushions is a great example of how to add color to a room without going overboard. I chose a white-painted finish for the chairs to liven up the existing dark table and add a contemporary note that would be missing with a traditional matching dining set.

RIGHT: When all the key elements in a room are unified by the same color, a sense of calm permeates. In the library, sage-green upholstery and walls painted in a complementary shade form a soothing envelope, punctuated by the owners' collection of colorful scrapbooks and journals. The space is perfect for solitary reading in the morning or having a cocktail in the evening with friends. I lucked upon the painting, which perfectly fits the narrow spot over the fireplace. **FOLLOWING PAGES**: The green-on-green color scheme creates a neutral backdrop and welcoming environment for any object that's put into the space, and my clients' extra-long painting was just the thing. It has a commanding presence and special meaning to them.

ART OF LIVING

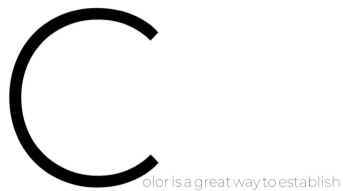

Color is a great way to establish links from one room to the next, but it's important to realize that an understated approach can have as much of an impact as room after room of dense, rich colors. For these clients, the owners of an elegant Georgian-style house with lots of classical detailing and paneled walls, I used a yin-yang approach. If you were to only look at the living room, which has white moldings, white walls, and ivory upholstery, you might say, "What color?" But the devil is in the details. Previously, the clients' coveted collection of artwork was lost against a sea of decadent red walls. I took the reverse approach and applied a neutral canvas as a backdrop and selected a few key colors from the paintings for the accent pillows, French armchairs, and curtain trim. That's it, but the impact is undeniable—the room reads as being filled with color. From there, adjoining spaces, such as the dining room, were treated to a more-is-more approach. At dinner parties, their prized Velázquez-inspired painting is the star of the show against the reflective blue-lacquered walls and the shadows cast by the dimly lit crystal chandelier and a table full of flickering candles. The color evokes a cozy mood and encourages conversation, and everyone feels as though they've been welcomed into a warm embrace—both in this room and throughout the house.

Indigo-colored walls in the dining room the view onto the grand foyer. In contrast, I left the walls in the entry white to add balance. It serves as the pathway to various other rooms that also feature distinctive color palettes. Having moments of clarity and relief that only white can provide is important in any decorating scheme. I replaced the original beige tile floors with marble in a classic checkerboard pattern in keeping with the home's Georgian vernacular.

When I first began working with these clients, I promised to keep their favorite art, rugs, and furniture, all of which was reupholstered. The walls were originally a deep red color, which actually distracted attention away from their collection of paintings. I chose to design the new palette around their artwork and use colors from certain pieces as accents, deploying them sparingly but judiciously on pillows, curtain trim, and the occasional armchair. Two large chandeliers were added to give this soaring space a more human scale.

Accent colors are like punctuation marks. Use them sparingly, but with purpose. French doors painted black define the entrance to the husband's study and highlight the room's architecture.

OPPOSITE: A pair of French armchairs is just one example of various blue hues used throughout the residence, and a faux-zebra rug breaks up the large expanse of wood flooring. FOLLOWING PAGES: The dining room is what I call an evening room, and the weight of the velvet curtains gives the feeling of being wrapped within a luxurious cloak. The artwork and saddle-colored leather dining chairs add to the intimate feeling.

RIGHT: Designing a very large kitchen island with room for storage below eliminated the need for upper cabinets. I chose to paint it in a rich, smoky blue, and hints of the color appear in the quartzite countertops and backsplash. The window mullions were painted black to resemble leaded-glass windows. Mixing stainless steel, chrome, and brass finishes on hardware and fixtures adds warmth and interest.

FOLLOWING PAGES: A limewash stain lightens up what were previously very traditional paneled walls in a dark finish. Simple linen curtains were all that was needed to frame the views.

People often shy away from bold color and pattern in a petite space, when in fact it can unify disparate elements. This wallpaper is a veritable kaleidoscope of inspiration.

Composed of various shades of red, green, and blue, the chinoiserie wallpaper is a riot of color and exuberant pattern in the petite powder room. The glamorous leather-clad door is adorned with nailhead trim for an additional accent. The burnished finish extends to the faucets and the hammered sink basin.

AS LIGHT AS AIR

I love spaces that take your breath away—or at least let you exhale. At this apartment I designed for a young family, the spectacular high-rise views do both, and my goal was to add a layer of design to simply complement that ethereal quality and enhance the beauty of nature just beyond the plate-glass windows. I don't design houses that are frilly or filled with froufrou touches, but I do love crafting pretty rooms, both understated and overtly colorful. Yet pretty doesn't have to mean old-fashioned. It was important here to balance softness with sophistication and avoid any saccharine accents that take a room from being well developed to over the top. In this apartment, twenty-six stories up, I embraced the cloudlike environment and even incorporated hints of pastel colors in an unexpected way. The pale blues and soft pinks here never would have worked had the furnishings been laden with superfluous detailing—everything is soft yet tight and crisp. Accessories are kept to a minimum. Stepping on the light rug feels like walking on a cloud. A vintage chandelier adds patina, while lacquered pieces add a gleaming touch as the sun shifts throughout the day. With vistas that stretch as far as the eye can see and a bird's-eye view of the changes that each season brings, this apartment is an ever-changing kaleidoscope of inspiration.

In a high-rise condominium almost thirty stories above street level, I created an ethereal, cloudlike ambience with billowing sheers that gently filter the natural light. The overscale mirror was designed to reflect daylight into darker interior spaces that don't have windows. The custom console features a pink geode accent reminiscent of a fabulous brooch, and the pale pink color of the stone recurs throughout the home. I think of this entire space as a jewel box in the sky.

The living room's neutral palette creates a dreamlike effect; beyond the barely there pink and icy blue accent colors on fabrics and artwork, there is little to disrupt the quiet vibe. The velvet-clad sectional was arranged to make the most of the corner unit's unique floor plan and take in the sweeping views.

Color is often dictated by place and time. For this high-rise condominium residence, a quiet palette echoes that of the surrounding skies and changing cloudscape.

The high-gloss lacquered ceiling is like a canvas—it picks up various colors throughout the day and at night, reflecting light from the ground below. The custom banquette and concrete-topped table were designed to fit into a challenging nook with an unmovable support column.

BLUE IS A NEUTRAL

Blue is a color that shows up often in my work, so much so that I'm surprised it's not one of the signature touches for which my designs are known. Icy tones, navy, cornflower, Prussian, midnight, teal, cerulean, robin's-egg—you name it—there's not a shade of blue I can't work into a decorating scheme, unless I'm limiting myself to a strictly white palette.

Sometimes I use one saturated blue to define a space, and other times, I deploy a collection of shades as accents to help make the room sing. In the foyer I designed for a charity decorator showhouse, several hints of blue show up in both a soft chinoiserie and a stark geometric patchwork pattern. Used sparingly, these colors add focal points at eye level (or below) to make a very vast foyer, complete with two dramatic winding staircases, feel more intimate. Because of their unique design applications—one atop twin ottomans and a throw pillow, another on a folding screen—they feel like their own canvases of artwork, albeit woven. The soft blue unified the three surrounding rooms created by other interior designers. Blue was the thread that linked all of us together.

In living rooms, keeping rooms, and dens, I've used blue fabrics in a variety of solid silks, velvets, and wools to help frame remarkable views as well as add architectural interest to unremarkable rooms. The dining room, kitchen, and powder room featured in this chapter showcase my affinity for treating blue as a neutral. This technique is most successful when it completely envelops a room or gives the illusion that it does, from the upholstery to the wall and ceiling paint to the moldings and window mullions—the more the merrier!

OPPOSITE: In a designer showhouse I participated in for charity, I was challenged by the need to create a unifying space in the foyer. Color was the solution, and blue was the common denominator, since the other designers in adjacent rooms had incorporated some variation of the hue in their rooms as well. I loved mixing the masculine Cubist print on the folding screen with the more feminine chinoiserie pattern on the sofa's pillow. Although not blue, the moss fringe edging, tufted cushions, and scalloped apron on the velvet settee are the types of bespoke details I love to use on neutral furnishings to give them extra appeal. **FOLLOWING PAGES**: A painting of Gloria Vanderbilt by Sally King Benedict was commissioned to incorporate hints of blue as well.

SUZANNE KASLER TIMELESS STYLE

BEAUTY AT HOME · AERIN LAUDER

SLIM AARONS · ONCE UPON A TIME

LIVING IN STYLE PARIS

STYLE BY SALADINO

VALENTINO THEMES AND VARIATIONS

Joys of life

KELLY WEARSTLER RHAPSODY

THE WORLD OF GLORIA VANDERBILT

RARE BIRD OF FASHION

Living in the Countryside

Bobby McAlpine THE HOME WITHIN US

The Houses of VERANDA Lisa Newsom

THE WORLD of MURIEL BRANDOLINI

SALADINO VILLA

VANITY FAIR 100 YEARS

FLORENCE
PARISIAN INTERIORS
LUXURY HOUSES TOSCANA
Inspired Styles
IN THE PINK
Palm Beach An Architectural Legacy
Magnificent Baths

The swirling design of the blue pillow fabric is reflected in the diptych above with its sensuous lines, as are the pops of mustard from other pillows. The heft of the navy blue wool curtains lends them a structural, almost architectural, feeling. I painted the curtain rods, hooks, and finials white so they would disappear into the background. A faux-fur throw completes the look.

When using multiple shades of blue in one room, such as this dining area, I often like to mix the selection of upholstery materials; this one features nubby linens, soft hide leathers, lustrous silks, plush velvets, and mohair.

ABOVE: For a client who wanted something personal in his powder room, we commissioned a hand-painted design of constellations set against a backdrop of the midnight sky.
OPPOSITE: Painting a kitchen blue cannot be done without considering the home's other spaces. I prefer darker colors in more formal city kitchens and icier tones at beach houses.

POOL HOUSE OASIS

I hope the joy of decorating comes through in all of the homes I design. It's something I strive for, and my clients say they feel the good vibes I channel into their rooms. I do know that when I have the opportunity to work on more intimate spaces, I am apt to incorporate more color, pattern, and whimsy. Similar to a powder room, these are the types of spaces you might not spend a lot of time in, so my clients are willing to let me push the envelope.

In this pool house on a grand estate, I wanted to create a different sense of emotion separate from the main house, which is more formal. I wanted being in this space to feel like being on vacation, imbued with the freshness of tropical island living (even though the nearest port of call is five hours away). Pops of preppy grass green and high-voltage orange, simple campaign-style director's chairs, and palm fronds, bird prints, and a Slim Aarons photograph offer transportive qualities. Even the chandelier evokes a grass skirt. While the rooms are indeed happy spaces, I kept them from becoming cheeky or juvenile by mixing in quality vintage accessories from the 1960s, lacquer furniture, and timeless woven grass-cloth pieces. The bold geometric pattern on the main rug keeps the space looking fresh and like a room from today, not a replica of one that was done sixty years ago. I love incorporating history—even the not-so-distant past—with contemporary motifs and colors to create something fresh and original. And, of course, joyful!

Although hundreds of miles away from the ocean, this pool house evokes a happy seaside disposition. I chose to incorporate fun and punchy citrus-tinged colors and strong patterns, but I kept the walls and curtains white so as to not overwhelm the space.

Even on a cloudy day, the vintage rattan palm-tree lamp and Slim Aarons photograph will transport you to a sunny state of mind. Note how the combination of rectangular, square, and circular shapes for the pillows accentuates the graphic pattern of the rug.

ABOVE: The punchy colors and abstract nature of the snake forms on the wallpaper give this room a playful demeanor. **OPPOSITE**: The large palm frond–patterned grass cloth in the bedroom forms an overscale trellis pattern. Painting this room the color of the curtain fabric would have been too intense for the space, but in this application, it adds just enough pizzazz.

When my youngest client ever—a high-spirited, fashion-forward millennial—turned to me to transform her tidy cottage at a moment's notice, I quickly got down to it. Work and travel obligations demanded a tight turnaround. Sourcing trips to antiques shops unearthed a treasure trove of vintage finds that were mixed in with her existing upholstered and storage pieces. There's a nod to the Hollywood Regency style here, and a glamorous blue-and-mustard color palette accentuates the other gold accents and brass accessories. The colors look even more striking against the home's white shiplap walls and painted floors. An assortment of sharp, leggy furniture is as stylish as this season's must-have stiletto.

Because of my client's age, it was important for me to help establish a home that would transition for her as her life evolves and her tastes change. Although she's currently single, a double vanity was added to the master bathroom. Space was allocated for being able to entertain and host dinner parties with ease. And high-impact art plays a big role here, too—room was left for future purchases, and being able to educate my client on how to choose key pieces was an unexpected but fulfilling exercise. The colors of these works will change the spirit of the home as her collecting habits evolve. As my client continues to add a mix of high and low pieces along with art that speaks to her, there's no doubt the groundwork established here will nurture a lifetime of connoisseurship. And if she ever outgrows this home, I look forward to working with her on the next chapter knowing that she already has pieces she can carry with her for a lifetime.

OPPOSITE: For a younger client's first home, I covered the room's original Sheetrock walls with shiplap. It's a subtle gesture, but one that adds architectural interest to a room where it was previously lacking. As a bonus, it is also a great blank canvas for her collection of art. A cobalt-colored sofa is an investment piece that my client can adapt as her tastes change or even if she moves to another home. The house is very private, so window treatments weren't required. **FOLLOWING PAGES**: The living room's furnishings are all about the mix of materials and silhouettes: Lucite, stainless steel, brass, and more.

ABOVE: Rather than hanging individual pieces scattered throughout a house with limited wall space, grouping the artworks together lent the collection a touch of gravitas. OPPOSITE: The swirls in the graphic marbleized painting are a great counterpoint to the angular chandelier and the iconic twentieth-century table and chairs.

CALM

I design a lot of houses near the water, both by the sea and dotting the shores along some of the most picturesque lakes you can imagine. In these homes, which are often devised as places of respite for the owners and their extended families and friends, everything is designed to put the eye at ease. These are the rooms that let you take a deep breath and allow your shoulders to relax. That sort of "ahh" feeling is what I want visitors to remember from these houses, and hopefully they'll take a piece of it with them when they lock the door and head back into the real world. More than noticing the sofa or the chandelier, that feeling of security and comfort is paramount.

But even if your home isn't near the ocean and the idea of vacationing at home is appealing, the spaces in this chapter evoke that vibe on an everyday basis. In lieu of a lot of furnishings and accessories, fewer objects are used on a grander scale so that the visual impact is strong but not distracting. The key is to keep everything from becoming too matchy-matchy.

Abstract art is often incorporated for its contemplative qualities. Homeowners can gaze at an oil painting, a photograph, or a mural and lose themselves in it. The reflection isn't asking them to solve life's great questions—they've left those challenges at the office. From the upholstery to the paint colors, white-on-white palettes immediately create a calming effect. Even if all-white interiors scare you, don't fret: the current generation of high-performance fabrics keep spills, dog prints, and everyday wear and tear from adding any angst.

I have an arsenal of subtle devices I employ in these less-is-more spaces, but I actually love it when they go unnoticed. Placing TVs at a lower height is easier on the neck. Lowering light switches for ergonomic reasons just feels right. Creating "clean" ceilings is very important—reducing the number of recessed fixtures and vents and moving alarm sensors to a less prominent space gets rid of so much unnecessary visual clutter. That sort of cacophony is subliminal, but it is noticeable. Once they're removed, people may not even realize they're not there, but they'll feel the difference. Perhaps most importantly, the moments that evoke nature are what define these meditative rooms and encourage daydreaming, reflection, and nurturing. These are homes with heart.

A LIGHT TOUCH

Sometimes a home's challenges lead to the most rewarding results. This weekend home near the ocean was graced with beautiful architecture, but its footprint was only thirty feet wide, so we devised a plan for it to live in a much larger way than it appears. Once past the gracious but stalwart Dutch Colonial facade, the home looks inward: all of the ground-floor rooms open onto a beautiful interior courtyard, complete with a pool. Accordion-style doors open to the soothing sound of the water, which reverberates throughout the house. Light floods into the rooms. The same concrete paver flooring used outside continues seamlessly indoors, blurring the lines between inside and out—its porous properties help catch sand from the nearby beach. The furnishings, too, are suitable for the rigors of wet swimsuits and muddy paw prints. The dining room chairs were designed for exterior use, so a guest wrapped in a towel after a quick dunk in the pool can dine without worry. Slipcovered upholstery allows for easy cleaning. Organic touches echo the indoor-outdoor vibe, and reclaimed beams were left raw and unsealed, adding a rustic touch. Woven Balinese baskets used as giant pendants accentuate the home's tall ceilings. Since this home is a weekend retreat and time there is precious, the goal is to make life simpler, down to the tiniest of details. Floating shelves in the kitchen seemingly hover, keeping things light and airy, and the lack of cupboards means my clients don't have to search for something they need. Bowls and plates—almost everything—are in sight and within arm's reach.

The transition between indoors and out is seamless with Peacock Pavers flooring both in the foyer and beyond the entry. I loved the texture of this basket, and I knew it would be just great wired and transformed into a light fixture. Even at night, a warming light bounces off the cool Venetian-plaster walls.

RIGHT: From the living room, retractable folding doors open up to reveal the courtyard, which becomes an extension of the interior living space, with its cooking and dining area beyond the pool. **FOLLOWING PAGES**: The stylish woven dining chairs were designed for outdoor use, but their ability to dry quickly—from a wet towel or bathing suit—make them ideal for use inside, too. The simple stair railing is reflective of the home's Cape Dutch exterior architecture.

Even utilitarian spaces can be designed with nurturing characteristics. The lack of upper cabinetry afforded space for a window, allowing sunlight to stream through. The pale-wood finishes imbue the room with spa-like tranquility.

OPPOSITE: Woven textures flow throughout the house, in both dramatic and subtle ways. Each of the four counter stools features a woven-leather seat, while the sculptural pendant fixtures above the island were fabricated out of fish netting. All of the cabinetry is stained in a soft washed-oak finish, and open shelving keeps essentials close at hand. **FOLLOWING PAGES**: My clients' only request was that everything be light, bright, and comfortable. That quality is nowhere more evident than in the upstairs landing, where a plush sofa invites lounging and long naps.

COASTAL SIMPLICITY

For this couple, who purchased a fifteen-year-old beach home as a weekend getaway, it was fun to explore how they would use the space compared to their primary residence some 300 miles away. The owners are an active, health-conscious duo who were moving to a community where they already knew others, so making the home conducive to entertaining was on the checklist. The two also have a giant Great Dane. With all this in mind, everything had to be designed so that there wouldn't be concern about a spilled glass of wine at a dinner party or dirty dog prints after a morning jog on the beach. High-performance fabrics swath everything. Meditation and clean eating are also integral parts of their lifestyle, so creating that oasis of calm for introspection was paramount. There isn't any contrasting artwork to distract, nor patterned fabrics or superfluous accents, but there is an ever-present connection with nature. Light fills the space through simply adorned windows, and doors open onto an expansive second-story wraparound porch that provides a bird's-eye view of the Gulf of Mexico. I converted an extra bedroom into a media room to provide a space for them to relax and recharge from their busy life. I love creating houses that can change and adapt as my clients' needs do, both in the long term and at a moment's notice. This house can feel both intimate and extroverted depending on the mood, and that's why designing around a lifestyle, rather than a trendy paint color, will always create the best house.

OPPOSITE: I immediately knew these large handmade paper sculptures would be perfect for this stair hall in a house at the beach. Their shapes and silhouettes remind me of sand dollars, coral, and sea urchins, and I like how the angular lines of the white frames capture their fluid shapes. There's a lot of depth and dimension, yet everything is white on white.
FOLLOWING PAGES: Since the balcony was designed with a deep overhang, I chose to forgo curtains to let in as much light as possible. The main living area is on the second floor, so privacy isn't an issue either. The gentle, swooping curves of the fireplace I designed remind me of the graceful lines in Cape Dutch architecture.

From the fabrics to the paint colors, white-on-white palettes immediately create a lulling effect. These are the rooms that let you take a deep breath and allow your shoulders to relax.

The dining area is part of the main living space and was created with casual entertaining in mind. When the doors are flung open, guests grab a seat at the table, in the living room area, or outdoors. Putting a built-in banquette under the window freed up more floor space and made it possible to accommodate more people than individual chairs would.

I usually create dark spaces for TV or lounge rooms. This space, however, gets used throughout the day, so I chose a lighter, sand-colored palette. I used heavy fabrics, such as chenilles and velvets, and a fluffy shag rug to give it the same cocooning effect. Bunching a trio of chaise longues together is an interesting twist on a traditional sofa or sectional. They are extremely comfortable, and everyone can claim a personal spot of his or her own.

The mix of raw and earthy textures adds a Zen feeling to a room by connecting it with nature. A spa-like aura offers a transportive experience without having to leave home.

I wanted to create a mood in this bedroom that was as light as air. I kept everything to the barest essentials but didn't sacrifice on comfort or style. Each piece was chosen with purpose based on its design integrity. Upon going to sleep or waking up, the owners find themselves in an oasis of calm. Natural textures give the space a resort-like ambience.

BEACH RETREAT

I recently worked on the redesign of a twenty-year-old house with exquisite bones and a free-flowing floor plan. While I didn't knock down walls to reconfigure rooms, I did rethink each of their purposes. For starters, everything was very dark. The stained hardwood cabinetry, floors, and staircase and moody paint colors didn't contribute much levity to the house, even though it's located just steps from the ocean and features a soaring, light-filled three-story stair hall. The original formal dining room was far removed from the kitchen, so I flipped that space with the living room. The now-adjacent kitchen and dining spaces have become more of a gathering area for the type of informal at-home entertaining people do today that wasn't so commonplace two decades ago. The new living room, a space that had previously rarely been used, has now become a family favorite. It seems as though the more carefree the room, the more people want to gather in it. Swaddled in sheers, the space is an elixir for long days spent in the glaring sun. Swivel chairs, an L-shaped sectional with chaise longue, and down cushions encourage the notion of doing nothing except deciding whether to move out onto the pool's sundeck chaises and linger under the shadow of palm trees.

OPPOSITE: When a new pool was added to this home, I specified a ledge inside it so there's room to relax, partially submerged, atop chaise longues. It's the ultimate resort-like detail. **FOLLOWING PAGES**: Organic touches in the living room appear in the oversize photographs of agave plants, the seagrass rug, and the bleached-driftwood table. The light-as-air sheers dance as ocean breezes pass through. Everything was specified for the ultimate in comfort—even the chairs swivel with ease.

Rethinking the home's original layout, I decided to turn the former living room into the dining area. Now that the dining area is next to the kitchen, both spaces are more conducive to entertaining. The elongated bell lanterns from Morocco accentuate the three-story-high stairwell. Vintage bamboo director's chairs feature white vinyl seats and backrests.

The kitchen cabinetry was originally painted a moody harvest-gold color, not really ideal for a carefree beach house. A coat of white paint transformed this room, uplifting the spirit of the entire space. As with the director's chairs in the dining room, the original built-in banquette was reupholstered in white vinyl for ease of cleaning.

COLLECTED

Creating rooms that are layered and feel welcoming but not cluttered can be tricky for the best of us. There's a very fine line between the two. I often think of Coco Chanel's famous saying about dressing and accessorizing your wardrobe: "Before you leave the house, look into the mirror and take one thing off," she advised. It's counsel that stands the test of time, and I attempt the same idea with my interiors (although admittedly, it's easier to trade out a bangle bracelet than a lampshade).

In order to create layered rooms that aren't staid or stifling, I imbue them with fanciful decorative moldings, formal family heirlooms, personal collections, and patina-rich antiques. Every element must be curated and deliberate. There's a high level of detail in the spaces I design, but not a fussiness or an overdone quality. There could be a museum's worth of fine art on the walls, stacks of exquisite china in the cupboards, and a mountain of down pillows atop a sumptuous bed, yet the art is simply framed, not in elaborate gilt surrounds; the china is the quietest of porcelain but can be used every day; and those pillows most likely feature subtle edging details in lieu of the frills of tassels and trims. Simply put, there is restraint in the abundance, and every room has space to breathe so that the owners can continue to add their own layers of history.

I recently read that people are more interested these days in collecting experiences rather than objects. I believe my clients are buying fewer but better things and that they still want to bring a part of their adventures home with them, whether they've been to a far-flung exotic locale, an antiques show, or a flea market or tag sale down the street. Sometimes it's just about creating a special canvas for them to compile their memories or enough negative space for them to fill in the blanks. In any case, the tapestry of their lives should be fully represented, and I'm here to facilitate their journey in a way that's both meaningful and without pretense, but also stylish and edited.

CLASSIC CHIC

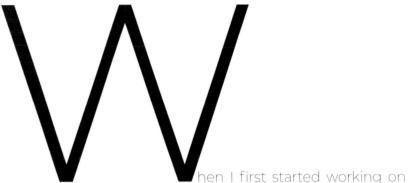

When I first started working on this milestone project with a couple of longtime clients—they're young entrepreneurs, but we've already collaborated on two previous residences together—I was presented with a conundrum: I was getting to work on a 1934 landmark residence designed by legendary architect Philip Trammell Shutze, but the home had been the recipient of a recent addition that contributed little to its pedigree. Thankfully, the two-year journey that ensued allowed me to both honor the home's stature and give my clients a house that echoes their vibrant spirits. They've become stewards of a home that is beloved by many, and the pressure was on to do both of them justice. Thankfully, many of the original doors, fireplaces, and moldings were intact, while the new addition benefited from thicker doorjambs and other detailing to better connect it to the original structure. We even relocated the existing kitchen and added a new pool pavilion and terraces for improved flow.

We wanted to give the house a more colorful, fresh look that still suited its classical architecture. Hand-painted wallcoverings, patterned carpets, lacquered cabinetry, dazzling hardware, and bespoke lighting were soon commissioned—zippy flourishes appear from room to room without abatement. The signature tiger-print velvet sofa is a veritable calling card for the home's unmistakable high-style vibe. Amethyst-colored accents, pink onyx, and even orange, aqua, and pistachio hues seamlessly coexist side by side. We tried to make it look effortless, but having clients brave enough to say yes to the exuberance was only part of the story. They were dedicated to using the best materials and finest artisans, which allowed this vision to become not only a reality, but also part of the enduring legacy of this important residence.

OPPOSITE: This home's stalwart Regency-style architecture is offset by my clients' youthful verve and energy, which reverberate throughout the fashion-forward interiors. **FOLLOWING PAGES**: The tiger-print sofa was based on an iconic piece that once belonged to style maven Lee Radziwill. Its selection set the tone for the rest of the home, which is filled with colorful and glamorous details.

RIGHT: Any traditional design elements, such as the sparkling crystal chandelier and scenic wallpaper, are juxtaposed with contemporary touches. Amethyst-crystal lamps and dining chairs upholstered in a similar color liven things up. Even the formal drapery cornices, based on an antique design, feel fresh with their simple tape outlines. **FOLLOWING PAGES**: Unexpected pops of color appear on the family room's yellow French Moderne–inspired chairs (left) and the pistachio-colored contemporary sofa (right). To showcase the artwork, I chose to keep the curtains and walls the same white.

150

RIGHT: Part of a recent relocation, the kitchen respects the historic nature of the home with classic brasserie-style brass detailing. Instead of a traditional all-white kitchen, which could have been too stark, I chose a warmer cream-colored paint for the cabinetry and used crisp white subway tiles for the backsplash, accompanied by a pistachio-colored range and vent hood. The effect is subtle, but it keeps everything in the room from feeling brand-new.
FOLLOWING PAGES: The walls and ceiling in the wife's lounge are lacquered in a romantic peachy-pink hue; gilt outlines add dimension to the beautifully paneled walls.

RIGHT: Parchment-clad chests serve as nightstands in the master bedroom; I chose them for their hefty scale, which is in keeping with the soaring Louis XVI–style canopy bed. **FOLLOWING PAGES, LEFT**: A small niche created the ideal spot for a reading nook. I designed the cabinet to serve as a sleeping area for their small dogs. **FOLLOWING PAGES, RIGHT**: Dazzling starburst pendants hover above the onyx-clad island in the wife's closet, where everything is dipped in the same rosy hue.

Pink and green is a classic, all-time-favorite color combination. This guest bedroom is my take on it, albeit in watermelon and coral tones. The hand-painted watercolor-inspired wallpaper has an organic, abstract pattern, making for a backdrop that's both dramatic and soothing.

RIGHT: The husband's lounge, formerly the kitchen, was designed for languorous evenings at home, so I enveloped the space in a rich green tone to encourage guests to settle in. The bar is always stocked, and friends are welcome to make their own drinks. Built-in banquette seating provides a great perch to take in the action at the pool table. **FOLLOWING PAGES**: The pool pavilion, complete with upholstered sofas, was outfitted with the same rigorous attention to detail as the interior spaces. I even suspended a mirror above the built-in console to reflect the lush garden views.

Sometimes just one thing can bring an entire room together; here, it's art. This contemporary photograph unites the chartreuse accents on the upholstery and window treatments with the lush garden views just outside.

I wanted the breakfast area to feel crisp and tailored. Subtle flourishes include the banquette's decorative tufting and the Roman shades edged with a barely visible trim. I used vinyl to upholster the white furniture for ease of cleaning.

ABOVE: Animal-print fabrics are a timeless addition to any home, and I'm particularly drawn to the lines of the tiger pattern used on the sofa. OPPOSITE: In the powder room, a striking hand-painted mural creates a welcoming and unexpected surprise; its gold-and-black palette makes a lasting impression.

PATTERN PLAY

Before the first furniture plan is drawn, you have to know what's important to you. With my clients, often it's tricky when they've acquired a new property and haven't lived in it for any length of time (or perhaps they haven't even moved in). Almost always, how they live will be different from how they were accustomed in their previous home. New furniture and new floor plans excite them but can be daunting.

For these clients, with whom I helped renovate a 1920s-era home, getting the mix of old and new right was of utmost importance. With a young family in tow, any formality—like the grand entrance hall and sweeping foyer—had to be tempered with a contemporary spirit. It's certainly not a casual house, but there is an air of carefree elegance that sweeps throughout.

In the foyer, the mood is immediately set with a graphic black-and-white checkered floor that features an unexpected inlay detail reminiscent of a domino. The grand, sweeping staircase has a contemporary, ombré carpet (pictured on page 2) that shifts in color as you ascend to the second level, both fresh takes on classic design. A mix of decorative styles flow through the house—a marriage of different eras keeps the home timeless. Neoclassical and Regency furniture is juxtaposed with 1970s-era Murano-glass chandeliers and chevron-patterned carpets, and an Art Deco vibe fills the dining room with a goatskin dining table, coffered ceilings, and mirrored verre églomisé chests. Even the kitchen hints of a favorite French bistro or patisserie with charming café chairs, a minty-green banquette, and graphic tile floors. An edited palette of quiet blush and soft champagne colors allows this cross-cultural mix of styles to live in a world of harmony.

I wanted to place a mirror by the door to both amplify light and provide a place for quick self-reflection before leaving the house, but a solid expanse of reflective material would have been overpowering. By designing a mirror with an antiqued finish and horizontal bands, I was able to create a piece with more character and architectural integrity. The skirted ottoman was built to be just tall enough to stash shoes underneath.

ABOVE: I find it challenging to hang art on curved walls, so for this stairwell, I designed a bas-relief plaster wall with an Art Deco–influenced pattern. **OPPOSITE**: The graphic floors, which remind me of dominoes, are a contemporary twist on the classic black-and-white diamond pattern. **FOLLOWING PAGES**: Detailed millwork was added to the living room's walls and ceilings to give the space more complexity and rigor.

Collecting—whether it's of art or other objects—makes people happy. A prized piece will always evoke fond memories.

The marble fireplace mantel is free of ornate carvings but was designed with an exquisite bronze-inlay detail that adds to the room's understated elegance. The painting is by Todd Murphy, whose work my clients collect. The lines of the silk-and-wool chevron-patterned rug lead the eye from one end of the room to the next.

I designed a pair of tall folding screens to anchor one of the living room's multiple seating areas, and I love the interplay between their bold scale and the dainty mirrors. The gray, blush, and champagne palette unites disparate furnishings with unique silhouettes.

RIGHT: I used numerous pairs of objects throughout this house, such as the mirrors and verre églomisé chests in the dining room, to play up many of the spaces' symmetrical proportions. The parchment-covered dining table is eight feet in diameter, so I needed to select equally substantial chairs to surround it. Wavy chocolate-brown velvet stripes add interest to what otherwise would have been empty expanses of chairbacks. The flooring is French parquet. **FOLLOWING PAGES**: The breakfast area (left) and scullery (right) are both imbued with the feel of a French bistro.

Parallel rows of subway tile-clad barrel vaults give the kitchen a heroic, industrial vibe, and I designed barstools to echo the arch of the steel windows. Concrete-tile floors and hefty pendant fixtures ground the space. A whimsical porthole in the door lets the owners peer into the scullery (and lets light in, too). This same brass detail is reflected in all of the cabinetry hardware.

A zigzag carpet pattern and serpentine lines on the parchment chest are two motifs in the wife's study that give the space movement. The built-in desk, coupled with Lucite chairs, was created as a spot for the children to do their homework.

On the terrace level, the glamorous media room has a decidedly 1970s vibe with chocolate-velvet walls and a gold mirrored fireplace. The room divider is a vintage screen that I had refinished and retrofitted for the space.

The playroom was reconfigured to serve as a nursery; it will revert back to its original use when the children are older. The whimsical tented ceiling is actually formed out of plaster that was painted. A subtle grosgrain trim wraps around the perimeter of the room and accentuates the scalloped detail.

ABOVE: The terrace-level mudroom is anchored by graphic concrete-tile floors. The striped carpet leads to the kitchen landing, where I grouped the family's collection of black-and-white photographs in one area. **OPPOSITE**: Lavender and amethyst accents populate the daughter's bedroom. The scalloped detail on the bed canopy and Roman shades also appears on furniture elsewhere in the space.

ABOVE: The dazzling powder room is defined by its sparkling mirrored surfaces and vintage Murano-glass light fixtures. Black-and-white terrazzo floors and black-lacquered doors with hand-painted gold accents add another layer of glamour. **OPPOSITE**: The husband's bathroom pays homage to early twentieth-century European baths found in the grand houses and luxury hotels of the era. The marble wall is one solid slab and accented with Art Deco–style frosted-glass sconces.

COOL

I love visiting museums and art galleries, both near home and when I travel internationally. Sometimes I am inspired by the white gallery spaces as much as the pieces on display, but I particularly love an exhibition space that recedes and lets the objects on view really shine. Translating that ethereal feeling I admire into a residential interior is tricky, as I don't want to end up with a cold, sterile space. In the homes that are minimal in design, it's important to imbue them with a real sense of warmth and belonging—even if it's primarily composed of a neutral palette. Subtle flourishes reveal themselves the longer you linger in a space when your eye has a moment to examine the quiet touches and bespoke details. Even when color is employed, it is deftly integrated to cast a different mood, accent a key piece, or create a dance among shadows and perspective.

Upon closer inspection, the hand of the maker is evident in many of the decorative elements I employ. Tailored gauzy sheers waft in the blowing wind, luminous plaster finishes applied by a master finisher practically glow, and the soft touch of a handwoven cashmere throw feels as smooth as silk.

As a result, the furnishings in the space feel like art: the curved leg on a sofa might evoke a Brancusi sculpture; the finial on a curtain rod could be mistaken for a piece of fine jewelry. Because of the edited selection of furnishings and accessories, each takes on greater importance. Organic touches—such as stone, wood, and tile floors underfoot—add another layer of warmth. Other "rough" textures, such as woven rattan chairs, reclaimed-wood beams, and nubby upholstery, are paired with brilliant surfaces of brass, mirror, and glass, so there's a remarkable juxtaposition between the rusticity of natural materials and the high glamour of bespoke details. It creates an effect that is both timeless and very cool indeed.

CHIC RETREAT

The art of surprise is something that's lost with today's open-concept floor plans, where everything is often on view all at once. That said, I do love the conviviality these spaces offer, and I design for them often, but there's a lot to be said for cozy rooms and the privacy they afford.

Because this beach house is sited on a postage stamp size lot, it is quite vertical and each floor is composed of a warren of intimate rooms. As a result, each story reveals an array of idiosyncratic details, and one encounters more and more personality with each passing step up the dramatic spiral staircase. As always, I'm looking to give all of my projects a sense of place without being overt. In the foyer, I chose to create a sense of the shore by designing a pebble floor in a compass pattern. The central space is now considered the home's North Star. The two contrasting stone colors offer a dramatic effect, are soft underfoot, and nod to the ocean nearby. The circular staircase echoes the less-is-more approach, as well: it's a sculpture unto itself and evokes a sleek nautilus motif as it winds its way up, up, and away.

What's not so obvious at first glance are the subtle details that keep the eye from being distracted. The luminous reflection from the plaster walls creates an ethereal effect, while a lack of upper cabinets in the kitchen keeps the attention focused on the remarkable backsplash and its Moorish detailing. It's like the proscenium at the theater or orchestra. Dining at the kitchen island becomes a live performance that everyone can join. In the master suite, the arabesque pattern is carried into the bathroom's millwork and onto the raw-hemp headboard. Those subtle repetitions of form and pattern channel a chill boho vibe while being firmly rooted right at home.

OPPOSITE: These Venetian-plaster walls are literally cool to the touch, a welcome respite from the sun after a day at the beach. The foyer's pebble floor is not only attractive but functional: its crevices are great for capturing the last specks of sand from sandals and feet before it gets tracked throughout the house. A V-groove pattern on the hardwood door is accented with bronze rivets to break up the expansive plane. Paint was diluted with water to allow the wood grain to show through and give the door a soft patina.
FOLLOWING PAGES: The bleached-teak-root cocktail table feels as if it could be a piece of driftwood washed ashore from the beach just beyond. Oversize pendants are suspended over the dining area by rope and mounted with nautical cleats that enhance the seaside aura.

PREVIOUS PAGES, LEFT: Woven hemp pendants cascade down the plaster stairwell. **PREVIOUS PAGES, RIGHT**: An abstract painting by George Williams is a beautiful backdrop for the French armchair and rush-and-teak console—the polished finishes of both pieces evoke the sleek wooden surfaces often found on yachts. **ABOVE**: The overscale wooden chain is a tongue-in-cheek nod to dropping anchor at the shore. **OPPOSITE**: The Moroccan-style ogee arch is the first example of a shape that is echoed in several elements throughout the house; here, it's a gracious gesture that frames the beautiful veining in the Calacatta marble backsplash. **FOLLOWING PAGES**: The gracious motif reappears on paneling in the master bath (left) and on the woven muslin headboard in the master bedroom (right).

WANDERLUST

I love incorporating global influences into my interiors, but it has to be in a way that doesn't feel forced or out of place. For this beach house, fashioned after a traditional riad, I was able to channel some of my favorite motifs from Greece, North Africa—Morocco, in particular—and Spain. The Mediterranean flourishes worked well in this residence, not only because of its own locale in a hot, sunny climate, but also because the home's complementary architecture was designed to usher in the much-needed ocean breezes.

A private courtyard entrance blocks all outside noise, and a long, intimate passageway seemingly carries you into another world. Almost every wall and ceiling surface is crafted in white plaster, which creates an instant cooling effect. Avoiding imitations or derivatives of a culture's style is what makes this project a success. Every piece is grounded in authenticity. The low-slung sofa, with its rolled arms, is truly Ottoman Empire in style. But instead of an ornate jacquard or embellished fabric, a simple white linen allows it to beautifully integrate into the overall scheme. Abstract paintings and decorative pottery recall favorite moments from the Cycladic islands and the French Riviera. A custom brass chandelier in the dining room casts a constellation pattern at night, evoking evenings under the Saharan stars. The Moroccan tiles on the kitchen backsplash are the most literal use of materials from that area, but anything else would have felt like an unnecessary trick. A plaster Gaudí-inspired octopus fireplace surround in the master bedroom is as transportive as the underwater seascape mural in the adjoining master bath. The subtle references to water hearken back to vacations well spent and are subtle nods to the never-ending inspiration that travel offers us—and the enduring appeal of incorporating those memories back home.

In the entrance of a beachfront home built in the style of a traditional Moroccan riad, the reverberating sound of water pouring from the copper scuppers into a small pool has a transportive effect. The ceiling is covered in pecky cypress, a rough-hewn material that I love for its imperfections.

ABOVE: A painting by Sally King Benedict captures the joys of beachside living through the artist's whimsical brushstrokes that suggest the energy of the waves and sun. **OPPOSITE**: To add texture, I created slipcover "sweaters" with overscale tassels for each of the iconic Panton chairs. Aglow at night, the custom Moroccan chandelier casts a constellation of pattern across every surface in the room, bringing dinner under the stars indoors.

A Moroccan-tile backsplash creates a striking focal point in the airy kitchen. Plump barstools suggestive of chic chess pieces add a touch of whimsy. After all, weekend homes should be fun! To keep sight lines minimal, I added a lot of storage into the design of the kitchen island, including plenty of drawers at the end near the dining area. Keeping silver, napkins, and other accessories nearby makes entertaining a breeze.

When designing a room, ask yourself, What is essential? From there, search for unique pieces. This bed, nightstand, and lamp offer stylish takes on the most basic creature comforts. What else do you need?

OPPOSITE: A Sally King Benedict wallcovering provides a soothing backdrop in a guest bedroom. Keeping furnishings low to the ground, including the woven pendant light, plays up the height of the room's tall ceilings. The channel-tufted headboard echoes the curves of the lacquered nightstand—I believe such subtle repetitions of form help create a soothing environment. **FOLLOWING PAGES, LEFT**: Dramatic plaster details accentuate the walls in the master bedroom. **FOLLOWING PAGES, RIGHT**: The octopus fireplace surround is inspired by the designs of Catalan architect Antoni Gaudí.

OPPOSITE: A covered daybed on the bedroom porch—ideal for afternoon naps or even sleeping outdoors at night—is a cosseting room within a room. **ABOVE**: Vacation homes should afford the opportunity to escape, physically and mentally. I love including elements of fantasy in my designs, such as this hand-painted mural depicting an underwater seascape. The geometric pattern of overlapping ovoid shapes on the floor was created by mixing Thassos marble with brass inlay.
FOLLOWING PAGES: Water plays an important role in the design of any riad, especially the private interior courtyard. One of my favorite features here is the waterfall design—there's a built-in bench in the pool for relaxing underneath the cascading curtain of water.

BEACH BEAUTY

I always love to put a spin on the classics. Blue and white is such a beloved color palette. After all, what's not to like? It's a tried-and-true combination, both timeless and comforting and simply pretty. You can't go wrong. At the shore, where this home is located, it is often the de facto scheme for crafting a beachy look. To put a contemporary spin on it and not fall into any expected clichés, I chose to channel a 1970s verve to liven things up. I was growing up in Florida and California during part of that era, and the essence of beachside living has had a lasting influence on my work, from the way the light is reflected in the sea spray at dusk to the soft, wet sand underfoot at high tide.

Here, I started with a white paint color as the basic envelope. There are expansive planes of materials, but I created warmth by using a driftwood stain on the floors, ceilings, and kitchen cabinets, along with billowing sheers to create texture and curved doorway arches that soften the edges. I actually chose to incorporate blue quite sparingly, but in each instance that I employed the color, it is with quite a punch. The den is the only public space to feature a saturated color, which I chose since the room is primarily used in the evenings as a space to watch TV, and it feels like a cocoon. A pair of his-and-hers iconic Womb chairs by Saarinen echo the sentiment. Elsewhere, I used various shades of the hue in unique ways: on the statement pendants, in an ombré effect; atop a coffee table, in a shagreen finish; on the range and hood; and on a custom cabinetry stain in a powder room. Using the blue in these ways is totally unexpected and unorthodox, yet the applications feel as comforting and familiar as ever.

A driftwood wash covers both the wooden floors and ceiling in the living room. Most of the spaces on this floor are in an open-concept floor plan, so the entrance to the den was imagined as a proscenium arch, leading one into a quiet inner sanctum. Although the space isn't completely separate from the adjacent rooms, sheers can be closed for additional privacy. Because the den is elevated, it affords choice views of the nearby ocean.

The den is a cozy space used primarily in the evenings for watching TV. A shaggy white wall-to-wall carpet contrasts with and balances the deep midnight-blue tone of the walls and seating. Books are displayed with their spines to the wall, giving the shelves a sculptural effect and minimizing visual clutter.

Ceilings are often overlooked. Try covering an expansive space with beautiful wood paneling for texture and warmth. Wallpaper or an unexpected paint color are also savvy solutions.

Large tapered metal pendant lights, with each colored ring undulating in an ombré effect, add definition to the dining area in the open floor plan. Using the same wood as the floor, the ceiling was designed in a parquet pattern that helps break up the expansive plane. The abstract artworks, painted on untreated linen, have organic textures and complementary tones that unify the ceiling, the floor, and even the console below.

RIGHT: The range hood is covered in glass that was painted on the reverse in a beautiful shade of periwinkle. Paired with a matching range in the same color, the wall becomes an altar-like focal point. The color extends onto the cabinets in the scullery just beyond. Most kitchen islands have seating on one side, but the capacious design of this home allowed me the opportunity to place counter stools on both sides—better for conversation! **FOLLOWING PAGES, LEFT**: I wanted the bed in the guest room to have presence but not be overpowering. This brass-and-Lucite marvel makes a strong architectural statement yet almost disappears at the same time. **FOLLOWING PAGES, RIGHT**: The covered outdoor porch is a favorite gathering spot and place to take in the spectacular sea views.

ABOVE: The master suite's pale sea glass–colored walls reflect a feeling of serenity, and I swaddled the canopy bed in linen sheers in the same color for continuity. **OPPOSITE**: The room's adjacent sitting area is a favorite place to relax. The ivory carpet and vintage French furnishings make it one of the wife's preferred spots for repose. Rather than add additional color, I used barely there textures for interest, from the shagreen cocktail table to the quilted, Chanel-style fabric on the stool.

ABOVE: While most of the rest of the home is light and ethereal, I chose to turn up the intensity in the powder room—a space where one doesn't linger for very long. The design was about exploring a range of textures in deep, rich hues with little contrast—from the wood grain of the cabinet drawers to the inky blue wallpaper to the rich blue pattern of the marble countertop. **OPPOSITE**: A similar treatment was used in the bar area, where I layered a dramatic work of art over an even more robust wallpaper. The beauty is in the cacophony.

ACKNOWLEDGMENTS

Thank you to my loving family, Stanley, Colin, Harrison, Cydney, Jeffrey, and Lucy, for all your support and understanding, and for giving me the ability to pursue my dreams. And especially to my Stanley, for giving me such beautiful canvasses.

I will always be eternally grateful to my Welsh family and especially to my grandparents, Enoch, Florence Jane, Edwin, and Lorna Patricia. To my forever-young parents, Lucille and Colin, thank you for showing me how to love, nurturing my independence, and letting my creative spirit soar.

Thank you to every member of my fabulous team, whose dedication, energy, and love of design makes coming to work every day a joy. I am particularly grateful for Jill Tompkins and Cristi Rajevac and their loyalty. Special thanks to Katie Runyan, Hannah Altmann, and Hanalee Lowry. To my friend and partner, Debbie Bagby, thank you for making our store in Big Sky, Montana, a reality. To Karen Gardner, my office manager and assistant, without whom I could not have accomplished what I do.

To all the artisans, craftspeople, workrooms, builders, with whom we collaborate to create each project, your thoughtfulness in the design process makes everything better. We could not have done it without you. Here are a few...

Artists: America Martin, Mario Soria, and Richard Olsen, all through TEW Galleries, Sally King Benedict, George Williams, Paige Kalena Follmann, Todd Murphy, Peter Keil, Pablo Picasso, Ruud van Empel, Trine Søndergaard, Hendrik Kerstens, Kevin Archer, Eleanor Driver Post, and Matt Kleberg.

Craftspeople/Workrooms: Source, LLC Atlanta, Karpaty Cabinets, Bjork Studio, Bradley USA, Douglass Workroom, Byron Conley Wallcoverings, Bethany Travis at Penshaw Hill, and Willard Pitt Curtain Makers

Builders: Benecki Homes, Cole Construction, Ladisic Fine Homes, Helenbrook Custom Contracting, t-Olive Properties, Earthbuild, Alcon Construction, and Alys Beach Construction

Architects: Pak Heydt & Associates, Ruard Veltman Architecture, Bill Ingram Architect, William T. Baker, Andre Tchelistcheff Architects, Howard Design Studio, Land Plus Associates, Stainback Hess Studio, A Boheme Design, Domin Bock Architects, T.S. Adams Studio, Studio A Architecture, Lewis Crook, Philip Trammell Shutze

To all the editors who have been supportive of my work and have brought my career to new heights, I thank you for being so gracious to publish my work: Lisa Newsom, Dara Caponigro, Clinton Smith, Carolyn Englefield, Ann Maine, Jill Waage, Sophie Donelson, David M. Murphy, Pamela Jaccarino, Kate Abney, and Elizabeth Ralls.

My sincere thanks to my publisher, Charles Miers, and to my editor, Kathleen Jayes, of Rizzoli International Publications for believing in me and for making my dream come true. To Doug Turshen and David Huang, thank you for your guidance and ability to create something from nothing.

Extra-special thanks to my agent and friend, Jill Cohen, who could see that I was ready and was the guiding force in making this book a reality.

I am eternally grateful to Clinton Smith, who from the beginning encouraged me and unknowingly helped me develop my subsequent career. Your beautifully written words bring such life to my design projects, and your guidance and attention to detail throughout this entire process has been one of great wit and wisdom.

Special thanks go to my photographer, Mali Azima, who has captured the true spirit of my spaces from the beginning.

Finally, to my lovely clients, who have so generously and trustingly allowed me to practice my art: thank you. None of this would be possible without you.

First published in the United States of America in 2021 by
Rizzoli International Publications, Inc.
300 Park Avenue South
New York, NY 10010
www.rizzoliusa.com

All images by Mali Azima, except pages 87, 88-89, and 91
by Emily Followill

Publisher: Charles Miers
Senior Editor: Kathleen Jayes
Design: Doug Turshen with David Huang
Production Manager: Barbara Sadick
Managing Editor: Lynn Scrabis

Printed in China

2021 2022 2023 2024 / 10 9 8 7 6 5 4 3 2 1

ISBN: 978-0-8478-69725
Library of Congress Control Number: 2020947629

Visit us online:
Facebook.com/RizzoliNewYork
Twitter: @Rizzoli_Books
Instagram.com/RizzoliBooks
Pinterest.com/RizzoliBooks
Youtube.com/user/RizzoliNY
Issuu.com/Rizzoli